THE [AUTHORIZED]
Ben Treasury

THE [AUTHORIZED] Ben Treasury

BY JOHN TROY

WILLOW CREEK PRESS

Minocqua, Wisconsin

ISBN 1-57223-011-8 Softcover
ISBN 1-57223-010-X Hardcover

Published by WILLOW CREEK PRESS
              an imprint of Outlook Publishing
              P.O. Box 881
              Minocqua, WI 54548

For information on other Willow Creek titles,
write or call 1-800-850-WILD.

Printed in the U.S.A.

AUTHORIZED PAW PRINT

Contents

SPRING

"It's *only* a checkup!"

"Who ordered all this stuff from the fishing catalog?"

"Ben, does the term 'Ice out' ring a bell?"

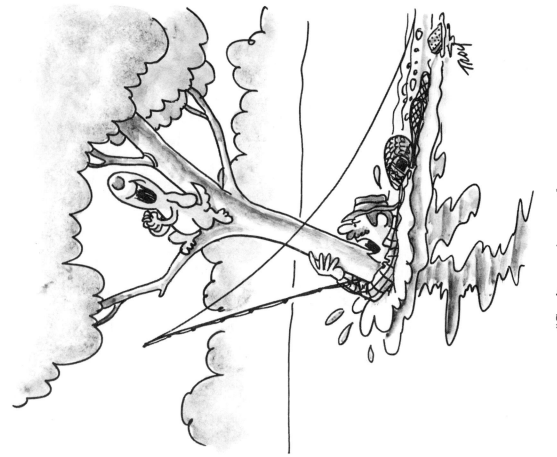

"Can't you sing another song besides 'Old Man River'?"

"Spring must be coming, Ben's getting a little strange with his teddy bear."

"Don't you know any other song besides 'Singing In The Rain?'"

"I never saw anybody make such a fuss over a Spring checkup!"

"Nice lure, Ben. Make it yourself?"

"HEEL! HEEL!"

"Do you mind?! I'm trying to fish!"

"Why can't he be afraid of thunderstorms like other dogs?!"

"That's $10.00 for Ben's physical, $7.50 for the rabies shot,
$22.50 for the pants, $14.95 for the shirt..."

"We're here to fish, Ben, not spawn!"

"When it comes to waking up hibernating bears, Ben, you've got Mother Nature beat by a mile!"

"Well, I wouldn't go so far as to call it a *vicious* attack."

"I sent Ben to fly fishing school, now he's a menace to the *whole* stream!"

"Ben's discovered that using a frying pan for a landing net cuts out a lot of unnecessary moves."

FLY FISHING ONLY

"Nice try, Ben, but that's *not* a fly rod!"

"Ben feels if you have to net them anyway, why bother using a rod?"

"Yessir, Ben us fly fishermen answer to a higher calling."

"Everybody misses a fish now and then, Ben. Once you can accept that, I'll turn you loose."

"No, Ben, making your eyes go bigger *does not* make the fish grow bigger!"

"There! A little starch and *voila! An Easter Bunny!*"

"Ben has a new fishing technique—he calls it 'Fish Hawk'."

"BEN!"

"The only neoprenes that fit Ben were gloves."

"You don't have to worry about muggers around here!"

"I really don't think mouth-to-mouth works on fish, Ben."

"Uh-oh, Ben, remember that guy you told to 'Get rid of that
coffee grinder and learn how to fly fish?' Well . . ."

"Somehow an electronic fish finder just isn't as exciting as a 'Ben fish finder'."

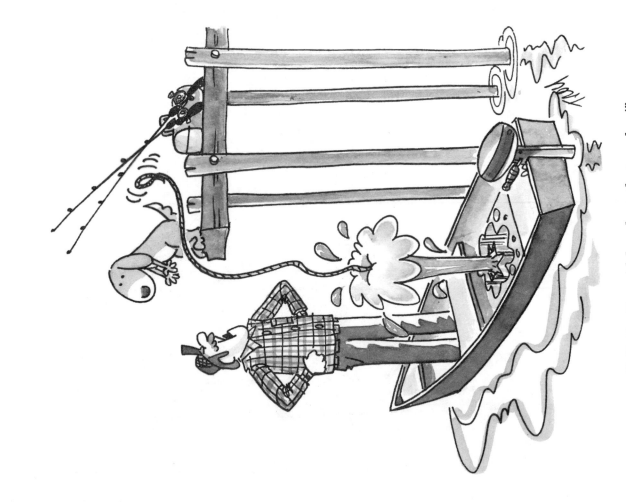

"I distinctly said *hand* me that anchor!"

"You're not really that much help, Ben."

"I'll be darn glad when your mail-order waders get here!"

"Yes, my Gretchen is in season—but a lot of good that will do little Ben."

"I take it you're not into catch-and-release yet, eh Ben?"

"Wow, for a mountain stream this sure has a lot of *toads* in it!"

"Sometimes I feel sorry for these little baitfish, don't you, Ben?"

"Ben, true sportsmanship is a state of mind, and I'm proud of you!"

"At least he isn't into drugs."

"Ben's taking fly fishing lessons. There goes his instructor now."

"I'll give five bucks to anyone showing me a fish more than ten inches long."

"Ben's idea of small game is that miniature collie next door."

"Wow, what a monster! Hang on, Ben, I'll get the net! No, no, the gaff! Wait! The *harpoon,* yes, the harpoon!"

"So don't keep forgetting the net!"

"My, my, Ben, look what our neighbor has brought you for Father's Day."

"Part of retrieving, Ben, is knowing when to let go!"

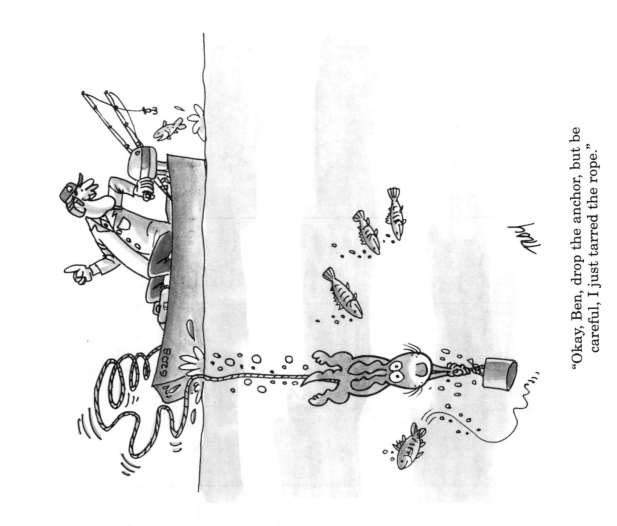

"Okay, Ben, drop the anchor, but be careful, I just tarred the rope."

"C'mon, Ben, there's no need to *count them out!*"

"You find it, Ben, you're the retriever!"

"It was easy teaching Ben how to fish. Now I'm teaching him how to quit. C'mon, Ben, *it's time to go home!*"

58

"So who needs sonar!?"

"You'll just have to make do until I can find your boot size."

"Better fish while you can, Ben, it gets a little rougher downstream."

"Ben believes looking suave is the most important part of fly fishing."

SUMMER

"BEN!"

"Ben, check that catfish bait and see if it's ripe."

"Can't you just hand me a plastic worm?!"

"Okay, lifestyles-of-the-rich-and-famous, start that motor and get us into some shade."

"Don't row so hard!"

"Now *cut that out!*"

"Hand me the mealy worms, Ben, they're in that container."

"Say, what happened to my plastic popping frog?"

"Uh-oh, it's a cop, and boy, *does he look mad!*"

"Wow, when you lose a trail, *you lose a trail!*"

"This is the *last* time I take you frog hunting!"

"That's funny, everybody else is going *down*stream."

"Ben's disappointed.
He thought it said 'stud.'"

"Ben wakes up when the ice melts, or for hunting season, whichever comes first."

"Now what, I ask you, could possibly go wrong on this picture perfect day?"

"Yes, I'd say Ben's approach to fishing is more 'direct' than it is 'classic'."

"It's *plastic,* Ben, it's *only plastic!!*"

"Who says fishing isn't an aerobic exercise, eh Ben!"

"So you think we can get away with one license this way?"

"Just keep howling till we get to the dock, Ben."

"The sonar finds *underwater* structure.
You watch out for *surface* structure!"

"Ben is now 'the compleat angler.'
Unfortunately, he can't move."

"Which reminds me, Ben, how many of my fish did you miss this year with your sloppy netting?"

"Give me your paw, Ben, *please,*
give me your paw!"

"You're going the *wrong way*, Ben!"

"What do you mean you can't wait for hunting season?
We're only halfway through *fishing* season!"

"He's got to come up for air sometime!"

"Do worms feel pain? Of course not!
As a matter of fact..."

"Fishing is Ben's life."

"When I said, 'Where should we go fishing today,' I meant where in this country!"

"Oh, no, he taught our bait how to shake hands!"

"Ben!! It's only spawning season for salmon!"

"So I said 'Give me a break, Ben, go swimming with your friends or something'."

"If you don't mind, I'll spot my own fish!"

"No, no, you idiot! The *muskie!* *HIT THE MUSKIE!*"

"BEN!"

"Come look, dear, Ben is so comical trying to catch that bee!"

"Any chance your fly will hit the water in the next fifteen minutes? I'm getting dizzy!"

"No, no, Ben, you don't retrieve *these* birds."

"Here Ben, Heel . . . c'mon boy . . . It's a long way home, let's go . . ."

"Keep a tight line, Ben, KEEP A TIGHT LINE!!"

"Up to now my water dish was a big bore."

"No, no, that's not what I mean by 'trim the motor!'"

"I'm not even going to look."

"If netting fish was an Olympic event, Ben would be a sure winner!"

"Ben had it custom built. He gets to all the good spots first."

"Look, wise guy, while we're in the city there are certain laws!"

"I'd like to think I've been some *influence* in your life."

"It didn't start out this way."

"Be forewarned, Ben is into sushi."

"Guess who got the most Father's Day cards?"

"Museum was broken into last night, Ben. Know anything about it?"

"On second thought, Ben, I'll just have them sunnyside."

"It didn't JUMP up there, you YANKED it up there!!"

"You're a hunting dog and you build a campfire *downwind* from a campsite?!"

"Ben is doing his bit for the environment.
He trees litterbugs."

"And all the while I thought you were *eating* your dry food!"

"Okay, okay, I'll take you camping!"

"'Hunting season is just around the corner'
is only a figure of speech, Ben."

FALL

"How about pointing them while they're still on the ground?!"

"What do you mean retired? You're only four years old!"

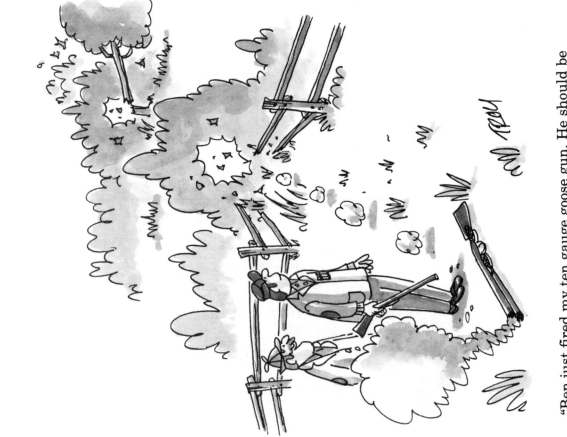

"Ben just fired my ten gauge goose gun. He should be coming back this way any minute now."

"... So begins the 'Fall' hunting season!"

"Ben won a blue ribbon in a field trial.
He hasn't been the same since."

"Jeez, could you wait until it hit the ground?"

128

"Want to squeeze a lifetime of hunting into one day? Go with Ben!"

"For gosh sake, LET GO so *I CAN LET GO!*"

"...and not only that, but air trapped between a retriever's dense coat and his body insulates him from even the most frigid water . . . are you listening, Ben?"

"He's either hit a hot trail already, or someone's opened a lunchbox in the parking lot."

"Now, that's a point!"

PHWEEET PHWEEET

"Now what does that game warden want? He's already checked my license."

"You never run out of 'missed again' routines, do you!"

"Uh-oh, Ben's 'wired' again, I better cut down on his high protein dog food."

"Don't mind him, he gets that way every Opening Day when I tell him he can't have a gun."

"Dogs gotta fly, birds gotta sing' isn't the way that old tune goes, Ben!"

"There's one thing about Ben, you'll never catch him begging."

"Why is that traffic cop blowing his whistle at us? . . . Uh-oh!"

"That's not what I mean by 'leading a duck', Ben!"

"*Now* what did you bury?!"

"That time of the year, eh Ben, don't know whether to go hunting or fishing?"

"I said *point, not poke!*"

"Shhh, Ben's running it right to us. That's his 'I've got everything under control' howl."

"Nice retrieve, Ben, But I'd like it to be on the same day I shoot it, or at least the same week!"

"Hooboy, here they come. Now's my chance for a double! 1 . . . 2 . . ."

"It's from our insurance company. They say if I keep hunting with Ben they're going to raise my rates."

"Looks like that pheasant got into the sticker bushes."

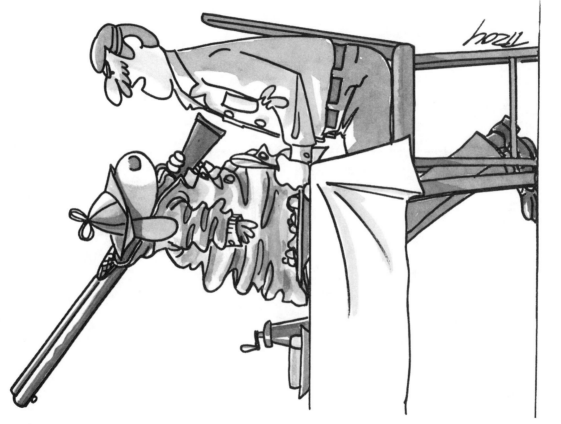

"I know hunting season starts tomorrow, so get out of my mashed potatoes!"

"Al, is your dog in season again?"

"Another bullseye! What do you think of black powder guns now, Ben?"

"How long did you say it was 'til trout season?"

"I'm sure looking forward to this mountain goat hunt. How about you, Ben?"

"Ben is out to settle an old score with a porcupine."

"Okay, so you're pointing. Now what?"

"The last thing I knew he was on a plane to an obedience school in Omaha!"

"What ever happened to 'point'?"

"I don't know what it is, but if Ben's afraid
of it, a shotgun won't do you any good!"

"When Ben hollers 'treed', you never know what to expect."

"You flush this one, wiseguy!"

"Ed says Ben is better at flushing birds than any dog he ever saw.
At the time, Ben was trying to point."

"I liked the old days when I'd pull you in the boat by the scruff of your neck!"

"Ben feels they mathematically improve his chances of flushing game."

"Looks like you're having a pretty good season, eh Ben?"

"Nice point, Ben. Any other bright ideas on getting us out of this mess?"

"There's not a mean bone in his body."

"Ben, you don't know how nice it is to be hunting with you, especially after fishing with you."

"You're not supposed to catch them!"

"You can at least *look* interested!"

"Did your shooting improve today, Dear?"

"We're not going to make a habit of this."

"We better start thinking diet, Ben."

"So Ben, how do you feel about helping Ed break in his pup?"

"Are you going *exploring* or *retrieving a duck?*"

"Here they come, Ben, look alive now!"

"I don't think his heart is in the game."

"Oh, Tom was supposed to go hunting with you today? Just a minute, I'll see if he's home."

"Don't you dare!"

"Take my word for it, they're easier to retrieve *after* I shoot!"

"... Psst ... heel ... heel Ben, psst ..."

"Who wants to go hunting? . . . c'mon boy . . ."

"Give the nice doggie his bird, Ben."

"I *see* it. *You're* supposed to *get* it!"

"He was born to the sea."

"... and just what do I tell the farmer, Ben, that you, a veteran hunting dog, winner of a state field trial, doesn't know the difference between a pheasant and a chicken ... is that what I tell him, Ben?"

"... without a moment's hesitation Lassie leaped into the rain swollen river ..."

"*Now cut that out!*"

"Oh, c'mon Ben, it isn't *that* bad!"

"That's it, Ol' Boy, the fire's dying, we'll have to fight our way out! Ben . . . oh Ben . . . ?"

"Whoops, another miss—but who's counting?"

"Why do I get the feeling of deja vu?"

"Now that hunting season is over. I'd suggest separate vacations."

WINTER

"First day of winter, get ready for a house guest."

"Uh-oh, we left the electric can opener plugged in!"

"What's this? 'Registered retriever stud service, your place or mine' then it gives our phone number."

"I don't want to name names, but somebody is howling off key."

"Why don't you develop cabin fever and go out for a run!"

"I don't think Ben wants to hunt anymore."

"Well sure, *you've* got brakes on *four* wheels!"

"Stay warm last night?"

"I don't know why I let you talk me into such hare-brained schemes . . . darn it, missed again!"

"If you think I'm going to keep unbuttoning you all day, you're crazy!"

"Yeah, sure, Happy New Year to you too, Ben."

"Don't worry, Ben I'll have us out of here in no time. Trust me."

"Ben doesn't know what to do between hunting season and fishing season, so he shot February."

"Let's go Ben, there's two feet of good tracking snow out there. Ben . . . Ben . . . Ben . . . ?"

"Worse case of cabin fever I ever saw."

"No, I'm not running rabbits past your snow fort!"

"FAIR-WEATHER FRIEND!"

"So let's see, if the groundhog stays out we'll have an early spring.."

"Don't worry, Ben, in the next chapter Buck tosses off the yoke of slavery by
escaping the ruthless French-Canadian trapper's sled dog team and
ends up in a comfortable home in the San Fernando Valley."

"Ben's idea of backing a point is to call and say 'nice job'."

"Quite the little beggar, isn't he?"

"That's funny, he was here a minute ago."

"How nice of you to drop in, and with Snookums, too."

"Uh-oh, Ben's practicing his ice fishing again."

"It's his moon walk. It looks like he's coming to eat his dry food but he's not."

"Ben, STOP PLAYING WITH YOUR FOOD!"

"Ben thought he needed more fiber, so he ate his blanket."

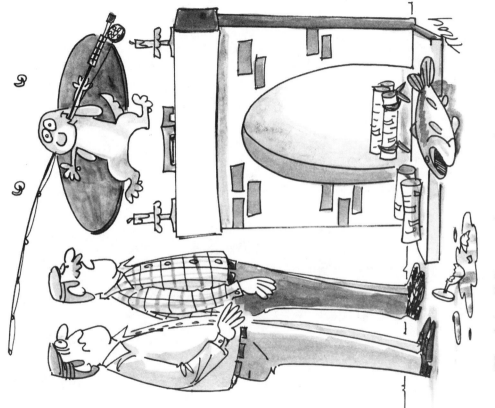

"Knock it off, Ben, you're scaring the guests!"

"Ben has his own cute little ways to show his dislike for dry food."

"Ben is disappointed. He thought the Wildlife Federation was a swinging party group."

"Now there's a dog who knows how to relax!"

"As you can see, Ben's fish isn't very big . . . Ben! . . . BEN!"

"Our neighbors say Egbert here is Ben's son, and it's okay if he visits us for awhile. They've retired to the Bahamas."

"Honey, did you put the Tabasco Sauce in Ben's dish by mistake?"

"Guess who netted it."

"Ben shot my gun twice. You're looking at the first time, and the last time."

"Will you look at this, Ben tied up his first fly!"

"*You tell me how he does it.*"

"Uh-oh, Ben's making his move on Goldie's food again."

"Hey Mister Petrie, what's the world's record for tennis balls in a retriever's mouth?"

"Stop doing walleye pike impressions while we're eating."

"Let's see, I can save four bucks on a license, 127 bucks on dog food, about 90 on vet costs..."

"Sorry Ben, I never noticed the baby-sitting clause in the stud contract."

"Dropped your pork chop? Kiss it good-bye."